I0560441

Rooted in faith, Raised by Education,

and Realized Through Enterpirse, A legacy

Forged by Two Powerful Women

From Country Roads

To CEO

By

Cheryl Harris and Dr. Brenda Scott

From Country Roads to CEO

ISBN 979-8-9990678-0-7

Copyright © 2025 by Cheryl Harris and Brenda Scott

All Rights reserved by Cheryl Harris and Brenda Scott. No part of this book may be reproduced by any reproduction method or form without prior permission in writing from the authors.

Scripture quotation is from the King James Version of the Bible.

Dedication

This book is dedicated to our parents, Cheryl Harris parents' are Mr. and Mrs. Joe and Bernadine Booker and Dr. Brenda Scotts' parents are Mr. and Mrs. James and Virginia Ruth McClerking who have gone on to be with the Lord.

They were visionaries who owned land and residential property back in the 1970s, long before generational wealth became a common conversation. They understood the power of ownership, the strength of legacy, and the importance of laying a foundation for those who would come after them.

Their foresight and faith paved the way for us, and now it is our honor to continue the journey they started. The legacy they built lives on in us, and through this book, we hope to pass that same wisdom and opportunity on to our children, our grandchildren, and to every reader ready to change the trajectory of their family's future. We would like to thank our parents for the blueprint, the example, and the love. We carry your vision forward.

This book is also dedicated to our children and grandchildren. We pray you not only embrace the legacy that has been passed down to you, but that you pick up the torch and carry it even further. The journey of generational wealth is not just about what we leave behind, it's about what you build, protect, and pass on.

You are the future, and the time to start is now. May this book be a guide, a reminder, and an inspiration as you continue the race we've begun with faith, wisdom, and purpose.

This book is also dedicated to our siblings. We are deeply grateful that we grew up in the same loving household, where our parents instilled in us the values of family, love, and preparation for life's journey. Together, we learned what it means to nurture, to support, and to rise. Your encouragement, love, and unwavering support have inspired us to grow and glow into the motivators and leaders we are today. Thank you for walking beside us, lifting us up, and believing in the vision. This legacy is ours to share.

This book is also dedicated to you, our readers. Whether you are renting or just beginning to consider the idea of homeownership, we hope to inspire and motivate you to take that first step toward building wealth and securing your future. We are honored to share our knowledge and experiences with you, and our greatest hope is that something within these pages help you move closer to your dreams and aspirations. May this book be a spark that ignites your journey toward ownership, legacy, and generational wealth.

Quote

"A Good Man leaveth an inheritance to his childrens children:" (Proverbs 13:22, Part A, King James Version)

Booker and McClerking
Generational Wealth

Joe Booker

James McClerking

B.F. Booker

Children

Joe Booker

Brenda McClerking
Scott's Wealth

Children

Cheryl Booker
Harris's Wealth

Children and
Children's Children

Children and
Children's Children

Table of Content

Preface

From humble beginnings on a country road to leading a thriving real estate company, I've lived the journey that proves the power of homeownership and now, I want to help you begin yours.

My name is Cheryl Harris, CEO of Harris Realty Services and FastTrack Real Estate School. With over 28 years of experience in the real estate industry and more than 70 agents working under my leadership, I've seen firsthand how owning a home can change lives. It's not just about having a roof over your head; it's about building something lasting, something that can create generational wealth, stability, and freedom.

One of my real estate broker and instructor for FastTrack Real Estate School wrote this book with me, and her name is Dr. Brenda Scott. Dr. Scott was a public educator just like me until I convinced her to join in the real estate industry before retiring. So, we have written this book with one clear mission: to educate, inspire, and empower individuals and families to understand the true value of owning a home. Renting may offer flexibility, but it rarely builds your future. Every mortgage payment you make as a homeowner is an investment in yourself, not in someone else's financial success.

Imagine this: by the time your child is ready for college, your home's equity could help cover their tuition without the burden of student loans. That same equity could fund a new business, purchase a vehicle, or even help you invest in more property.

These are opportunities that simply don't exist when you're renting.

Through this book, we will walk with you step-by-step to uncover the benefits of homeownership and how it can become the foundation of long-term financial success. Along the way, I'll share the real-world insights I've gained from teaching and training at my FastTrack Real Estate School alongside our team of six dedicated instructors.

Whether you already live in your dream home, are dreaming of buying your first one, or want to start investing for generational wealth, keep reading this book! We believe this book is for someone you know who wants to understand about building a better future for their family or wants to use their home to grow wealth.

This book is for them too!

Read it, enjoy it, please share it, and let's

take the first step together.

Cheryl Harris and Dr. Brenda Scott

Chapter 1

The Purpose Behind This Book

Our purpose for writing this book is to give our readers a head start to building generational wealth. What is generational wealth? We're glad you asked. It is wealth that our parents left for us and our siblings in the form of land. Back in the late 70s and early 80s our parents learned the value of land. Once they bought some land, they held on to it till death and at death it stayed in the family. They instilled in us if we ever bought some land hold on to it because one day it will be valuable to us.

Growing up in the country, we always knew land was something special. It was more than just dirt and fields. Our parents told us land is scarce, its value rarely depreciates, and when used strategically, it can open doors to financial freedom. Land was a foundation, a legacy, and a source of opportunity, but it wasn't until becoming a real estate broker and an agent that we fully understood its power.

Now, are you ready to take charge of your future and or your child's future; if so keep reading *From Country Roads to CEO.* Your journey to financial freedom and generational wealth begins now so let's get started.

Chapter 2

From Country Roots to Shared Dreams

We are Cheryl Harris and Brenda Scott. Born and raised as two country girls from rural Tennessee. Though we didn't know each other existed, we were unknowingly walking parallel paths, with hearts full of ambition and a shared hope for something greater.

In the 70s, both our families lived on a dirt road that led to a white two-story house, where we spent our early years with our parents and siblings. Living in those big houses in the 70s was a sign that we both had big dreams and ambition in our heart, even from a young age to make a difference in our life and the lives of others. Even as young girls, we dreamed beyond the walls of those homes, knowing deep down that our lives were meant for purpose, not just comfort. We didn't know exactly what that purpose looked like, but we knew we were destined to make a difference not just for us but for others too. Long after the dust had settled on those country roads and our paths crossed, we realized we both have the same values and the same dreams. It felt like we had known each other forever. What started as friendship quickly turned into mentorship, purpose, and a shared mission that neither of us could have imagined.

Although we were raised miles apart in little towns most people have never heard of even as of today, we can truly say the life our parents gave us shaped who we are today. Growing up, our parents taught us the value of hard work, resilience, and the simple joys of life which still remains close to our hearts no matter where we go.

This book is our story. It's about faith, friendship, perseverance, and the power of believing that no matter how small your beginning, your ending can be bigger than you ever dreamed. It's for anyone who has ever wondered if it's too late to pursue your calling, and for those who need a reminder that God's timing is always perfect even when we can't see the plan.

Welcome to our journey.

Chapter 3

Leading Harris Realty and Fast
Track Real Estate School

Hello I'm Cheryl and I became the CEO of Harris Real Estate Services, having over 70 real estate agents under my leadership in Tennessee and a few years later, I started my own Real Estate School along with co-founder Dr. Reginald Harris where I employ instructors to teach real estate classes for my company.

Real estate has been a blessing to me and my family. I'm a homeowner in the city, I have land in the country, and I am a developer of a few subdivisions. It's amazing what you can do and accomplish with BIG faith and BIG dreams. It just goes to show that anything is possible, with a dream and God on your side. I'm writing this book to show you that no matter where you come from whether it's a small country town with country roads, the wrong side of the tracks, or even the streets, real estate investing can teach you how to build wealth to pass down to your family. Therefore, your background doesn't define your future! I believe that where you come from is only a part of your story, not the whole book. Throughout history, countless heroes and accomplished individuals have risen from humble beginnings, proving that determination, hard work, and vision can take you anywhere. I carry that belief with me as I navigate my own path, striving to turn dreams into reality, traveling country roads and now I'm a CEO.

I'm writing this book with one of my

agents, Dr. Brenda Scott, an author. She too came from humble beginnings.

Chapter 4
What is Real Estate?

Real estate is land and anything built on it, like houses, buildings, or farms. It includes places where people live, work, and shop. Please read below only a few types of real estate:

1. Residential Real Estate – These are homes where people live, like houses, townhouses, condominiums, tiny houses, and apartments.
2. Commercial Real Estate – These are buildings used for businesses, like stores, offices, and hotels.
3. Industrial Real Estate – These are places like factories and warehouses where things are made and stored.

    People buy and sell real estate to

make money and a lot of money can be made in real estate. People often think real estate agents and brokers are rolling in the money. If you are a homeowner or become an investor in real estate buying and flipping houses or renting apartments then you too could be rolling in the money after learning how to play the game. Some people buy houses, fix them up, and sell them for more money. Others buy buildings and rent/lease them to people or businesses.

Real estate is important because everyone needs a place to live, work, and shop! So if you haven't purchased your first home yet, it is never too late to start now.

We understand nothing comes easy and it takes money to buy and invest.

And when it comes to finances and investing, many of us don't get a perfect start. So starting at a disadvantage of not having the money doesn't mean we have to finish there. As teachers, we didn't teach to get rich! It was because we loved children, sharing knowledge and helping others grow in knowledge. Every step along the way, we had to **learn, adapt, and dig our heels in to get a head start in life.** Today, our income is determined by our efforts, our hustle, and our mindset. **We don't wait for opportunities to come our way, we created them as we traveled on this journey.**

There are great benefits of being in real estate and yes, obstacles come our way as well but, we look at obstacles as a lesson for change. We learned that success is about positioning yourself **around people who are going somewhere and doing something.** You don't have to know everything all at once. Just have a willing mind to learn. We took the step to pay for classes and courses to learn more about real estate and investing that has paid off for us and we want to share that knowledge with you. Now, we live in a time where information is at our fingertips. There are no excuses not to educate yourself about finances, investing, and building wealth because you have the internet, podcasts, and online learning. So don't wait. **Position yourself for ownership. Position yourself for generational wealth. Position yourself and your**

family for freedom. Because the best investment you can ever make is when you invest in yourself and your future. The difference between where you are and where you want to be isn't luck. It's what you do with what you learn.

Another lesson we have learned is that **feet that are always moving and searching for an opportunity to grow and learn have a better chance of finding what it takes to move to the next level in life.** Success doesn't come to those who wait; it comes to those who **chase it down, work for it, and refuse to quit.**

So, no matter where you are in life at this present time, don't become comfortable. Growth is always a good thing, so keep pushing, keep learning, and keep searching for the next available opportunity to reach for greatness because the finish line is yours for the taking.

Chapter 5

Lessons from Granddaddy on Reinvesting

Growing up in Tennessee, I learned about reinvesting from watching my granddaddy, B.F. Booker, also known as Cap Booker, back in the 1960s. He had a sharp mind for building wealth, even if he didn't know all the modern terms like "flipping" and "investing." What he did know was the power of leasing to own, a strategy that helped him grow his property holdings over time.

I remember standing on a ladder, watching him fix up a house he planned to rent out. He understood that improving properties increased their value, and that renting them out created a steady source of income. Long before real estate investing became popular, my granddaddy was already practicing it. He knew that reinvesting money back into properties was the key to financial growth.

His wisdom went even further back. He bought land in the late 1800s, and now, in 2025, all my siblings and I still have a portion of that property. The older generation such as my dad always told us, "Never get rid of land" (J. McClerking, personal communication, 1989). They understood its value not just in terms of money, but also in opportunity. Land could be used to grow crops, generate income, and even serve as collateral for future investments. They knew how to borrow against their land to acquire even more wealth.

My granddaddy's lessons on reinvesting

and wealth-building have stuck with me throughout my life. His actions showed me that financial independence comes from making smart decisions, reinvesting wisely, and holding onto valuable assets. These are lessons that should be passed down to future generations, teaching them the power of owner ship, investment, and financial growth.

By learning from the past, we can build a better financial future. Just like my granddaddy, we can take what we have, reinvest it, and create lasting wealth for the generations to come.

Chapter 6

Instilling the Homeownership Mindset in Children

Owning a home is an important way to build wealth and stay financially stable. Think of buying a home like planting a fruit tree. The earlier we plant it, the sooner we can receive lasting benefits. Eventually, the tree begins to bear fruit, offering nourishment and even shade on hot days. In the same way, a home can provide comfort, security, and financial growth know as equity over time. Perhaps the most beautiful part is this: even after we're gone, the tree remains. It continues to bear fruit and provide shelter for the next generation. That's building generational wealth. Just like a home that has been taken care of, it becomes part of the legacy we leave behind to the next generation.

Teaching children about buying a home early helps them learn good money habits that will help them when they grow up. One of the key lessons to impart to children is that owning a home is not just about having a place to live; it is also an investment. Unlike renting, where monthly payments go to a landlord and builds the landlord wealth. By saving money, making smart choices, and learning about the value of homes, children can work towards owning a home in the future.

Financial Stability?

Homeownership is one of the best ways to build financial stability. It is believed that a home is your best financial investment.

Why, because the value appreciates if it is well kept. Years of paying on a home is like putting money in the bank but it's in the form of an asset. Let's say you don't have a rainy day fund setup but you have been making your monthly payments on time each month and you need to borrow some cash. A banker would probably give you a loan faster than a person who rents a home. Why? A home can be used as collateral to borrow money, homeownership shows whether the owner makes their payments monthly on time which shows responsibility, and your home can be used as collateral to get money. Homeownership is just a part of building generational wealth for our family. Generational wealth is what we want to leave and teach to our children, and the roadmap starts with teaching our children about earning money, spending wisely, and saving for big goals like buying a home.

The Value of Homeownership

When you own a home, your money helps you instead of going to a landlord or the person you're renting from each month. Every time you make a house payment, you build something called equity, which is the value you own in your home. Over time, homes can increase in value, meaning they can be worth more money in the future than the date you purchased the home. This helps homeowners grow their wealth. Let's look at an example of renting versus owning. A lot of times, paying on your mortgage is cheaper than paying rent (depends on the price of the home and interest rate). So would you rather pay someone else's mortgage or build generational wealth?

It Teaches Early Money Management

It's important for children to learn how to save and spend wisely at an early age in life. Teaching our children about budgeting, saving money, and understanding credit can help them buy a home in their early twenties. If children start saving a little of their money now, they will get use to planning for big purchases in the future.

It Teaches Saving for a Home

Buying a home requires a down payment, which is a large amount of money paid upfront. Therefore, children need to learn about setting goals and saving money over time. Their money is like a seed being planted in the ground and over time, something will grow from that seed. So teach your children that putting money in a

savings account or investing can help their
money grow. So, encouraging children to
save a portion of their allowance or earnings
from a young age can instill a habit of
financial responsibility that will benefit
them when they are ready to purchase a
home.

Understanding Credit and Loans

People usually borrow money to buy a
home, which is called a mortgage. To
borrow money, they need good credit.
Children need to learn that paying bills on
time and not spending too much on credit
cards will help them get a loan when they
need one. So, parents introduce the concept
of credit through real-life examples, such as
explaining how paying bills on time and
avoiding excessive debt contribute to a
healthy credit profile because a certain credit

score is essential for obtaining a mortgage. Teaching children about credit, how it works, how to build it responsibly, and the consequences of mismanaging it definitely will help prepare them for financial independence.

Being in the real estate industry for over 26 years, credit is one of the major setback for homebuyers. Young people get credit cards while in college and after graduation their credit is missed up because they don't pay the bill on time which stops most of them from buying a home in their 20s or early 30s.

Exploring Homes and Neighborhoods

It's important to teach children about the many different types of homes and architectural styles, such as brick, vinyl, ranch-style, and many more. Exploring a variety of homes can help children appreciate the diversity of how people live. By learning about the design, location, and condition of a home will help children know what makes a home increase in value. Children can gain valuable knowledge that will help them make thoughtful and informed choices about housing in the future.

Earning Money in Different Ways

Children should be taught and given the opportunity to working a public job before they turn 18. I can recall a client buying her first house before the age of 20. While working and paying bills on time, she had a credit history allowing her to buy a home faster. It's also good to encourage entrepreneurial activities such as starting a small business, freelancing, or investing which can provide additional financial resources for a home purchase as well. The more money they save and earn, the easier it will be to afford a home because, learning to diversify income sources fosters a mindset of financial independence and security.

Chapter 7

Early Financial Lessons That
Build Lifelong Success

When children get money as a gift, they usually get excited and want to spend it right away. This is a great time to help them learn how to save some, spend some, and maybe even start thinking about investing for the future. This will help them grow up focusing on spending rather than saving or investing. Today, social media surrounds us with temptations and feeding into a culture of immediate gratification. When some children receive money, their first instinct is often to think about what they can buy rather than how they can make that money grow. This lack of financial education at an early age can lead to poor money management skills in adulthood.

Back in the 1960s and 1970s, particularly in the rural South, black farmers exemplified financial independence. Many of these farmers owned hundreds of acres, making them not just agriculturalists but also business owners. Running a farm required the same financial insight as managing a store, budgeting, investing, reinvesting, and planning for the future. These farmers understood that building wealth meant creating opportunities for themselves and their families.

One summer, I had the opportunity to run a financial workshop for children, teaching them about money management. My goal was to instill the mindset that money should work for them rather than just be spent. I introduced them to the principles of earning, saving, and investing. At the age of 16, I had my own financial revelation when my brother gave me stock in Pepsi Cola instead of money. This experience opened my eyes to investing and the power of wealth-building.

Teaching children about financial independence is crucial. When children understand how to build wealth, they gain the ability to create their own financial security. They no longer have to rely on others to make a living. Owning property, reinvesting earnings, and making smart financial decisions allow individuals to establish stability and long-term prosperity. Putting money back into assets, such as homes or businesses, ensures future opportunities for growth.

My financial workshop catered to students from kindergarten through college, reinforcing the importance of starting young. Early financial education nurtures responsible money habits that can last a lifetime. If I could reconnect with some of my former students, I would bet that many of them purchased their first homes in their early twenties. Others likely began investing as soon as they secured their first jobs.

This message is for everyone, young and old. It is never too early or too late to grasp the concept of making money work for you. Financial education is the key to independence, and by teaching children these principles early in life, we set them on a path toward financial freedom and success.

Teaching children about homeownership helps them to learn how to be smart with money and it equips them with the knowledge and skills necessary to make informed financial decisions. By saving, understanding credit, and learning about homes, they can work towards owning a home when they grow up. Owning a home is a great way to build wealth and have a stable future and it is a powerful wealth-building tool that can provide long-term financial security and stability. Encouraging children to aspire to homeownership helps set them on a path to financial independence and prosperity.

Chapter 8

If the Bank Tells You, No Loan!
You've Got Options

Create Your Own Door. My mother, a woman of grace with a very humble and sweet spirit always told me, *"You can make something out of nothing and to use what's in your hand until you get what you need"* (V. McClerking, personal communication, 1985). That wisdom stayed with me for life. At the age of 12 years old, I used my mother's advice. If I saw something in the store I wanted but I didn't have the money to buy it, I made it. I discovered a spark within me, a creative spirit. Just like sewing, I used that same advice in buying real estate. I rented until I made the opportunity to own a home.

My father was a visionary. He told me, I

could never work for anyone but myself" (J. McClerking, personal communication, 1989). He was a go getter. As a hardworking farmer, he taught me to be strong, tenacious, tough, determined, creative, and innovative. Quite often, I saw how innovative and resourceful he was when it came to fixing or needing a part for his farming equipment. If he couldn't buy a part for his equipment, he built it. He didn't wait for doors to open, he created them. These lessons and skills from my parents helped me when I stepped into the real estate world.

Before I turned 25, my husband and I set out to buy our first house in 1989. The bank turned us down for our loan. But, I could hear my father's voice in my spirit: *"Don't stop with that answer from the bank. Keep persevering and find another way"* (J.

McClerking, personal communication, 1985). I didn't let that stop me. I told my husband we were going to buy that yellow house and we did without that one banks help. That was a beginning to our generational wealth building. I asked the owner to finance part of the loan, and with support from another bank and my parents, we bought that yellow house. That house wasn't just our first home, it was the beginning of our wealth-building journey.

In the 90s' we had built equity up in our first home. Then I used the equity in that first home to invest in another home in the country. Having the first house still and our country home, I invested in another home three years later. Later on, I built a home without a loan, I purchased some commercial property and waiting to develop.

It's like repeat and do it all over again. See, I told you paying on a mortgage will give you an opportunity to borrow from yourself and pay yourself back.

When the bank tells you no, don't accept no as an option. I can tell you what I did. I went to the owner and asked about owner financing a portion of the mortgage and I shared with her that I would make monthly payments to her. Back then, I asked my parents and they helped me out and then I went to another bank and got the rest of the loan. There are different types of loans you can ask for as well, conventional, FHA, and etc. Please make a loan officer your best friend. They can tell you of programs from the government that could give you a certain amount down for the down payment. I'm not a loan officer so my advice for you is to contact an agent and ask them to connect you with at least three if you don't know of a bank lender. Then you will have advice from not just one loan officer but many.

In 2003, I became an author and published *"Are you an Eagle Trapped in a Chicken Coop?"* One of my favorite lines (Scott, 2003) is "If there's no door make one!" The door wasn't open for me to buy my first house in 1989 and guess what, I made a door. Now, I encourage you to make a door to building your generational wealth. I could have walked away sad and disappointed and I did for a few days but, I didn't give up or stop there. I made my door to enter into homeownership because I've seen my daddy make his own open doors so many times growing up on our farm.

I'm telling you all of this to say, don't

rent too long or forever. Owning a home is like making a monthly deposit in your bank account each month. When you own, every payment is a deposit into your future. It's a foundation you can build on to level up.

Chapter 8 Key Points

Chapter 9
Start Now, Paving the Path to Homeownership

Now! Now is the time to start your journey into homeownership and building wealth. By now in life, you are either a renter or a homeowner. We all need a place to live and if by chance you are renting, every month, you are saying goodbye to money that will not help you out in years to come. What should you do first if you are a renter? First get a copy of your credit score. What does a credit score mean? It is a number given to people who make loans and bills and if a person pays their bills on time they should have a good score compared to people who are late on their monthly bills. What is a low credit score? It means a person hasn't done a good job paying their bills on time. If a person has a score lower than 600, they would want to work on improving their score before buying a home. Lenders I have spoken with speaks about the higher the score the cheaper it will be for you to borrow money from a lending institution. Most lenders like to see their borrowers with at least a score of 640. I have talked with some lenders who will work with a score a little lower than 640. If you don't have a 640 then work on getting it there. If your credit is not where it needs to be or you would like to increase your score, start with only one credit card. Each month, only buy on that card what you can and will pay off within a month. Make sure that balance is paid in full before the month ends and in a few months, you will see your credit score rise.

This book is not just our story; it's a

roadmap. Whether you're looking to break into real estate as an agent, invest in property, or simply take charge of your financial destiny, We are here to show you how to build wealth for your family. If you're ready to make boss moves, build generational wealth, and take control of your earning potential then let's get started.

That knowledge changed everything for us. We see real estate not just as a way to build wealth, but as a way to create opportunities for you and for others. By leveraging your home equity (cash built up in your home), you will find a way to generate more income, take control of your financial future, and help others do the same.

Book one, *From Country Roads to CEO*, in a series of 4, we would like you to read this book for understanding. We want you to know what real estate is and how real estate can help you build generational wealth. If you don't own a home, we want you to start the process as soon as you can. Please, don't do it without the assistance of a real estate agent. Real estate agents are professionals who know the market and watch out for your best interest. A real estate agent's job is to help you find a home you like and work with you on getting into that home. Real estate agents take the stress and worries away from you and work with you until the key is in your hand.

Being a black professional in real estate, I want people to know that as a professional, real estate agents keep your information confidential. There are ethics we have to follow in real estate or stand the chance of losing our licenses. Therefore, you can trust us to be on your team. We are looking out for our clients and real estate agents are your friend not your enemy.

Chapter 9 Key Points

_____

_____

_____

_____

_____

_____

_____

_____

_____

_____

_____

_____

_____

_____

_____

_____

_____

_____

_____

_____

Chapter 10
Why a Real Estate Agent Matters?

A real estate agent is a trained professional who helps people buy and sell homes. We take special classes and pass state and national test to make sure we know what we're doing. **It is important to understand once licensed in a state, we are able to sell anywhere in that state.** I have talked with a lot of people who only thought agents are limited in one area but, that is not true. **Another important point is you don't have to use the listing agent of a listed property as your agent to buy that property. You have the right to choose your own agent for any buy or sell transaction.** As real estate agents, we listen to what our clients want and do our best to find the right home or buyer. We work hard, often without getting paid right away, because we want to help people make good choices. Being an agent, we deal with a lot of paperwork to fill out for our clients. We understand contracts, know how to negotiate, and guide our clients to make smart decisions. They also follow special rules called a "code of ethics" to make sure they are honest and fair. Using a real estate agent can make buying or selling a home much easier and less stressful!

Chapter 11
Cheryl Booker Harris: CEO, Visionary, and Educator

For over three decades, Cheryl Harris has been a beacon of wisdom, compassion, and guidance, touching the lives of thousands through the power of education. Gifted by God with the heart of a teacher, she has dedicated her life to equipping individuals with both academic knowledge and essential life skills. From the classroom to the community, Cheryl has remained steadfast in her mission to uplift and inspire, serving as a guiding light for young people navigating life's challenges.

Her journey began as a high school science teacher in the public school system—a platform that allowed her to shape the future of countless students. From an early age, Cheryl understood that education unlocks endless possibilities, a lesson instilled in her by those who came before her. Fueled by this belief, she pursued and achieved both her Bachelor's and Master's degrees in science, proving that with perseverance and faith, anything is attainable.

In the classroom, Cheryl was more than a teacher. She was a mentor, a role model, and often a surrogate parent to students in need. Her charismatic approach to education captivated young minds, not only teaching them science but also instilling in them the resilience and faith required to overcome life's obstacles. She embraced the calling to be an Ambassador of Education, recognizing that true success comes from aligning one's life with God's purpose.

As she transitions from the public school system, Cheryl's passion remains unwavering. She is now focusing her energy on empowering today's youth and young adults with the biblical principles necessary to lead victorious lives. Her greatest desire is to see individuals step into the fullness of their God-given potential, walking boldly in their purpose with wisdom and confidence.

Beyond education, Cheryl has also built a remarkable career in real estate. As the Principal Broker at Harris Realty Service, she leads a team of over 70 agents across Tennessee, Mississippi, and Georgia. For 30 years, she has exemplified excellence in the industry, serving her clients with unwavering dedication and providing them with the highest level of service. Cheryl's commitment goes beyond transactions—she is a trusted advisor, a compassionate listener, and an advocate for those she serves.

Now, as a Real Estate Instructor, she continues to educate and inspire, equipping future professionals with the knowledge and skills they need to succeed. Whether in the classroom, the real estate market, or the lives of those she mentors, Cheryl Harris stands as a testament to the power of faith, education, and perseverance. Through her unwavering commitment, she continues to plant seeds of hope, guiding others toward the extraordinary future that God has designed for them.

Chapter 12

Dr. Brenda Scott: A Life of Purpose and Progress

I'm Brenda McClerking Scott and yes, I'm a country girl from a small rural area in Tennessee. Before my retirement at the age of 56, I was a dedicated educator, lifelong learner, and passionate advocate for growth and resilience. Raised in a small country community, I grew up in a home filled with love and strong family values. I spent my childhood on a 130-acre farm with my parents, two brothers, and three sisters. When I was five years old, my parents built a brick home, marking a significant milestone in my family's journey toward generational wealth.

I pursued my education with determination, earning two Bachelor of

Science degrees and a Master's degree from UT Martin. I furthered my education at Freed-Hardeman University, where I obtained my Ed.S. and Ed.D. Having knowledge about real estate gave me an edge to purchase over three homes, build a home without a loan, buying commercial property and waiting to develop it. Without that knowledge, I would have settled for just buying a home and living in it. Upon retiring from education, I sought new opportunities and found my passion in real estate. Enrolling in FastTrack Real Estate School, I connected with my Broker and CEO, Cheryl Harris. This opened a new chapter in my professional life.

We know that our story is so many of our readers' story. That our journey wasn't easy but being taught lessons about perseverance and commitment while living with our parents paved the road for us to build doors when one closed. In my twenties, I opened and ran several businesses which were successful but at that time wasn't my passion.

In conclusion, either you own or rent a home because we all have to live somewhere but we would rather for you to own than rent because owning is about building wealth for you and your family. We hope you enjoy our first book which is book one of a mini-series. So, please be on the lookout for book number two in the very near future. Also contact us by email to find out where we will be giving our next Homeownership seminar.

For Speaking Engagements

Please contact Cheryl Booker Harris
at 901-268-2321

Or

Dr. Brenda Scott at
731-614-5944

cherylbookerharris@gmail.com or

Scottbs419@live.com

Other Links

https://harrisrealtytn.online

https://www.fasttrackrealestateschool.org/co
ntact_us

Seminar Notes

_____

_____

_____

_____

_____

_____

_____

_____

_____

_____

_____

_____

_____

_____

_____

_____

_____

_____

_____

_____

_____

_____

Seminar Notes

Seminar Notes

Bibliography

King James Version of the Bible.

McClerking, James. *Personal communication*. 1989.

McClerking, Virginia. *Personal communication*. 1985.

Scott, B. (2003). *Are you an eagle trapped in a chicken coop?* Blitz Print.

www.ingramcontent.com/pod-product-compliance
Lightning Source LLC
Chambersburg PA
CBHW071346130626
46556CB00005B/2047